CONTENT MAPPING

*Unlocking the Power of Content to
Increase Engagement, Leads and Sales*

Henry Adaso

Dedication

In memory of Conrad Salvador.
A brilliant marketer in every way.

"All action results from thought, so it is thoughts that matter."
Sai Baba

Contents

INTRODUCTION

"It's too whimsical."

The words cut through the conference room like a record scratch.

Silence.

The music stopped.

The choir of creative exuberance could no longer muster a tune.

It was as if someone walked up to the thermostat and shut off the air. I could keep going with the analogies, but you get the point.

The client clenched his hands in a steeple, allowing his words to rest in the air like condensation. Everyone on the marketing team took turns exchanging glances. No one was eager to respond. The creative director contemplated a response but decided against it.

"Well, our goal was to resonate," the senior lead on the account finally chimed in. The client did not nod in agreement. The account lead took the cue and moved on to the next slide.

You could probably guess what happened next: the client never renewed his contract.

Here's the thing: the ad concept was creative. The tagline was concise and compelling. The ad portrayed happy models, smiling and having fun. In fact, some might say that it checked off all the items on a traditional list of content marketing best practices.

Well, except for one tiny but significant detail.

The issue with the creative was not a lack of creativity. The problem was ambiguity for whom the marketing agency designed the ad. It wasn't the creative director's fault. He did his job. He delivered on his task.

But there was no consideration of where the buyer was in her buying journey—what problems she needed solved and why. The content was for everyone and no one.

Put another way, the content did not match the customer's context. The creative and copy were sunflowers and butterflies, but the client was trying to reach people with serious and urgent health problems. The tagline was whimsical, but the client was hoping for something professional and trustworthy.

So, the creative director developed what he thought the client wanted—not what the client needed.

Sound familiar?

It's no longer enough to create content for marketing purposes. To get better results with content today, we must look at it through the lens of our customers. We have to map content to the intent and scenario of the people we hope to reach. When we understand intent and scenario, we have a better chance of creating remarkable content.

1

INTENT AND SCENARIO

"...and then to church; and there being a lazy preacher, I sleep out the sermon."
Samuel Pepys' Diary,
2nd November 1662
(Administrator of the navy of England and Member of Parliament)

In 1732, Benjamin Franklin began publishing Poor Richard's Almanack. Almanacs were popular books in colonial America. Franklin's included poetry, weather forecasts, and a dash of wit and cynicism. The annual publication increased Franklin's popularity and economic success, reaching 10,000 copies per year. Benjamin Franklin understood the power of content marketing.

The goal of content marketing has not changed much since the days of Poor Richard's Almanack. Content marketing is still one of the best ways to attract, engage, and convert prospects into customers.

The most notable change since Franklin's era is that we now have more access to information and technology to help us deliver better content.

Not Spaghetti Content

During my five-year stint as a music journalist for *The Houston Press*, I frequently attended live concerts. My job was simple: Soak in every aspect of the show—the performance, the audience, the arena—and file a report for an audience of music fans. Over time, I became aware of a simple, intuitive fact: no two concert venues are alike.

Every venue differs, not just in size or capacity, but also in application. For instance, stadium arenas are better suited for household names like Shakira and Rihanna. These venues seat more people and are perfectly outfitted for theatrical displays. Smaller venues, on the other hand, are ideal for upstarts and local acts. These artists don't yet have the clout to sell out large venues. Plus, local acts often benefit from the intimate vibe of a small crowd.

Every venue has a purpose. More importantly, it is designed for that purpose. Multipurpose venues are mediocre. This is also true in content marketing.

Content functions differently, depending on intent and scenario. Multipurpose content—the type of spaghetti content that seeks to appeal to everyone—does not work. When you think about your content marketing strategy, start with the question: "Who is this for?" As with concert venues, where basic elements such as lighting and aesthetics differ from act to act, your content goals and purpose must be tailored to the people you are trying to reach.

This is the underlying concept of content mapping: *Content functions differently, depending on intent and scenario.*

Actions Begin with Thought

Think back to the last time you bought a big-ticket item, such as a car or a new piece of furniture. It probably started with a thought ("I need a new couch"). Perhaps, you identified a concern ("My couch is worn out").

Next, you researched your options. You probably considered a handful of them and, ultimately, made a buying decision.

Consumers move through these different stages of the buying process seamlessly. Content mapping helps marketers mirror the journey with their content. People think and act differently as they move through different stages of the buying cycle. So, your content must align with their journey in order to be effective.

But we're getting ahead of ourselves.

What exactly do we mean by content?

What is Content?

Wikipedia defines *content* as "information or experience provided to the audience or end-users by publishers or media producers." I define it more broadly. Content is anything that tells a story. It doesn't have to be produced by a brand or media company to be considered content. People make content all the time. When you send an email, design a flyer or sing in the shower, that's content.

Here are examples of the different types of content you can create:

- **Blog posts** created around long-tail keywords.
- **Social media posts** to promote, engage and enlighten.

- **Videos** of your company, customers, or employees.
- **FAQs** that provide a direct answer to common questions.
- **Newsletters** or any compilation of your content served up monthly, weekly, or daily.
- **Webinars or Seminars** to engage and inform (in-person or online).
- **Podcasts** on relevant topics, from health and finance to hip-hop and one-star Yelp reviews.
- **Testimonials** to resonate with like-minded prospects.
- **Customer reviews** that affirm value and help illuminate opportunities.
- **Newsjacking** from the media attached to your brand's value proposition.
- **Culture posts** to mix things up, (e.g. candid shots, behind-the-scenes footage).
- **Case studies** to signal credibility in the sales cycle.
- **Live events** that provide you an opportunity to make your case in person.
- **ROI calculators** to help your people calculate the value of taking the next step.

What is Content Mapping?

Content mapping is the strategic alignment of content with the needs of your customers throughout their buying journey.

All Customers are Not Created Equal

Wouldn't it be great to design a marketing campaign that moves a prospect from "Eh, I don't know if that's for me" to "Yes, sign me up right now!"?

While marketing has always favored meaningful storytelling, messages have historically been mass targeted. Content mapping aligns relevant messages with strong data signals, helping us pinpoint the needs of customers throughout the buying process.

Marketing technology has advanced to enable ease of scale and personalization. You can identify strong leads from a pool of prospects, and then nurture them with sequenced content marketing efforts aligned with their needs.

Creating content without considering where your customers are in their buying journey is like going on a road trip without a map. Sure, you'll get somewhere; but you leave your destination up to chance. Marketing is too important to leave up to chance.

A Content Map vs. A Sales Funnel

It's easy to confuse a content map with a sales funnel, but they are *not* the same thing.

Both are important for different reasons. A sales funnel lays out the path your sales team expects your customers to travel.

A content map, on the other hand, lays out the buyer's journey from your customer's perspective. This is the primary distinction between a content map and a sales funnel.

Another distinction is that a content map outlines a framework of deliverables necessary to convert prospects. In other words, a content map is a lead generation tool. It is aligned with the prospect's intent and research needs.

How to Create a Content Map

So, how do you create a content map? I'll show you in just a few steps.

I want you to get maximum value from this book so you can quickly move to action.

Here's a snapshot of what follows in detail and with more specificity and examples throughout the book.

1. **Define your content marketing goals**

   Forget SMART goals and complicated KPIs at this point. Let's keep it simple. What do you want your customers to do? Do you want them to be informed? Do you want them to simply become familiar with your brand, so they'll think of you the next time a need arises? Do you want them to put you on a list of the brands they're considering for a purchase? Do you want them to buy right now? Depending on what you want customers to do, your content map will look completely different.

2. **Start with Personas**

   Personas are fictional representations of your ideal customers. A persona could be an aspiring business school student, a first-time car buyer, or an enterprise software procurement officer. There is no content map without personas.

3. **Map content to the buyer's journey**

   Customers travel through the buying journey in an ARC (Awareness, Research, Consideration) before making a buying decision. This is a very simplified version of what is also known as customer lifecycle stages. People go through these stages as they mull a new purchase. They'll often ask themselves questions along that journey, comparing and contrasting solutions and services as they go.

So, your content must be distinct and relevant to each stage. For example, you probably don't want to offer a discount to buyers in the awareness phase. It wouldn't make much sense since they don't even know if they want the product. In fact, they barely know your brand. A discount ends up being a waste of resources. Now, offer the same discount to a customer who has already decided to buy the product but isn't sure which brand to choose, and you've just lowered the risk factor in their decision process.

Conversely, repeating a product description when the customer is ready to buy is low-value content. Presumably, the customer already has this information and just needs a little nudge to follow through and commit to the purchase.

Marketing is like networking. Timing, alignment and interest can help or hurt your chances of truly connecting. Act accordingly.

SOCIAL BUTTERFLY

In marketing, as in social situations, timing is critical. Ponder the following questions:

- When do you introduce yourself to a stranger at a networking event?
- What's the first thing you'd say?
- How do you generate interest?
- Do you feel comfortable taking the conversation a step further? Why? Why not?
- How would you nurture the relationship after the event?

2

PERSONAS

"Your message should single out your prospect like someone being paged in a crowded hotel lobby."
Claude C. Hopkins
(Advertising pioneer and author of *Scientific Advertising*)

L et's start with a scenario. Imagine you're standing in front of a crowd of 5,000 people, ready to give a speech. You've been preparing for three weeks. The big moment has arrived, and you're finally ready to deliver your speech.

There's just one problem. You can only see the backs of your audience. You can't see their faces. They have no clue who you are. You have no clue who they are. You don't know if they're young or old, men or women. You don't know if they're paying attention or dozing off in the middle of your speech.

Sure, you could make some educated guesses based on their hair, clothing and body language, but you don't have the full picture. You only have a vague idea.

Now, imagine that this is an audience of your potential customers—people who raised their hands and said, "Yes, I'd like to buy from you." Is this vague picture enough to understand and meet their needs? Probably not. You want to know who they are, what they're interested in, and the best way to help them solve a problem. To do this, you need to develop a customer persona.

What is a Persona?

A persona is a fictional but realistic representation of your ideal customers. Think of your personas as characters in a novel. They have physiological and psychological attributes. They have feelings, fears and motivators. They're practically real people.

To walk and talk like your audience, you must first get clear about who qualifies as your audience. This is where personas come in. Your personas are at the center of your marketing strategies. Marketing without a persona is like selling hamburger to vegetarians. They'll never bite.

Three Types of Personas

There are three main types of personas you should know:

1. **The Primary Persona**: This is the ideal customer you would like to reach. Your primary persona is likely to have the greatest impact on your marketing outcomes. Your content should be designed with your primary persona in mind.

2. **The Secondary Persona**: After your primary personas, this is your next most important group of customers. They may be on the fringes, or maybe they buy less frequently—still, pay attention to them.

3. **The Influencer Persona**: This persona influences the buying decision but may not necessarily be the end user. You want to take their needs into consideration and modify your tone to resonate with them.

Why You Need Personas

Anyone can create multipurpose content. It takes courage to do the work required to develop realistic personas and tailor content specifically to them. Here are just a few reasons why it pays to do the work.

Personas make your customers real

With personas, you get to move beyond theory and company mantra. You get to solve real problems for real people. What's important is to understand what it means to be your customer. Personas help close this gap.

Personas help us develop empathy

Personas activate our empathetic faculties. If you've ever waited in line for hours at a bank or had to pay exorbitant ATM fees, you understand the annoyance a bank customer feels. If you've had to deal with a rude customer service representative, you understand the range of emotions that go through a customer's mind. If you've had to put a loved one in an assisted living home, you understand the tone and timing of the conversations that drive these decisions.

Personas inform your content mapping strategy

To know your personas is to know the content that will likely resonate with them. The process goes hand in hand with content mapping. If you wanted to sell purple hats to school-teachers, you must first deduce that your future customer is a schoolteacher who happens to like purple hats. Your persona is the tip card on your deck of cards. Get it wrong and the entire stack crumbles. Get it right and good things can happen.

Voice vs. Tone

As children, we learned to adapt our voice and tone to our audience. So, we didn't talk to grandma the way we might have talked to Little Mike.

Your tone and language change depending on your audience. You might be more "professional" when communicating with a client and more casual with colleagues, whom you've known forever.

Same thing applies to personas. By having one handy, you can quickly and easily identify the right tone for the right people.

Once you've determined your personas, try to establish the voice and tone that would resonate with each persona.

There's a difference between voice and tone. Voice is a core tenet of your brand identity. Tone is contextual. In other words, voice is who you are; tone is what you do.

Your brand voice should be consistent across all your touchpoints: print, digital, in-person, etc. Your tone can and should change, depending on the scenario.

For example, you might maintain a helpful voice with a dash of conversational tone while helping a customer trouble-shoot an order on the phone.

As Kevin Potts puts it, "voice is to climate as tone is to weather."

Examples of brand voice:
- Helpful
- Bold
- Informed
- Friendly

Examples of brand tone:
- Conversational
- Confident
- Proven
- Refined
- Considerate
- Honest
- Meticulous
- Engaging
- Ethical

Consistency is Credibility

Once you've identified the right tone of voice, stick to it when creating content for your persona. Don't start off sounding like Sales Susan and end up sounding like Sailor Sam.

Your voice should mirror your personas and their peers. For instance, a physician might use technical terms when writing to other physicians. A sales manager uses sales lingo, like "prospecting" and "closing the deal" when addressing other salespeople. A C-Suite persona speaking to other executives will use business terms that might not be suitable when discussing homework with a six-year-old. A fashion designer will use fashion lingo that demonstrates an understanding of style. Adapt your voice and tone accordingly.

Real Personas

In Greek mythology, Athena sprang out of Zeus' head, fully formed. Your customers won't always appear with such theatrical flair, but they should be realistic enough.

The job of marketing is to access the conversation taking place in our persona's head. If you could feel what your customers feel or access the conversation taking place in their head, what would you say in order to add value?

Persona development allows us to create characters and inhabit them without judgment. By so doing, we can add value to our customers.

Novelists travel to their characters' cities and try to walk in their shoes. They might frequent their favorite bars and restaurants and generally try to get a feel for their daily life. You don't need to take expensive trips or hire Hollywood actors in order to develop a realistic persona. Today, you can do this with data, anecdotes, and a dash of intuition.

It's an exciting challenge.

Embrace it.

Dramatize your persona.

- *Stage*
- *Lights*
- *Action*

If the dialogue is clunky, you'll know it immediately. If the characteristics are off the mark, you'll know it.

Try it right now.

Pretend you're your persona. Take her out to lunch. What is she grappling with? What problems can you help her solve?

What are her objections? What did you say that made her face light up?

In other words, try to convince *you* to buy what you're selling. It's not kooky; it's marketing.

When in doubt, back up and act it out.

The 3 Rules of Persona Development

Here are three rules to keep in mind when developing personas:

Rule 1: There must be empathy. The most important ingredient in a good persona framework is empathy. The persona building exercise requires that you step outside your own shoes and try on someone else's. And to walk in someone else's shoes requires a great deal of empathy.

Rule 2: There must be data. Persona development is *not* guesswork. It's informed by data and anecdotes. Begin by gathering data on your target audience. You can do this by conducting primary research or by purchasing existing data (secondary research). Combine the data with what you know about your customers. Your sales team and customer experience teams are great resources for vetting persona attributes. The magic formula is data plus anecdote.

Rule 3: There must be creativity. Persona development also requires you to be creative. You want your persona to be realistic—as real as a human being with real needs, motivations, and preferences. Put yourself in the shoes of a novelist. Push your creativity and you might be surprised by how much you enjoy the process. Yes, it's a job, but it's just as important for you to have fun with the persona exercise.

Where Do Personas Come From?

The first step in the persona development process is to gather intelligence. You can do this in several ways:

1. **Primary Research**
   Conduct a survey of your current customers and prospects to understand their pains, priorities, and motivations. Analyze the data and use the information gleaned from the survey to develop realistic personas. Feel free to name them.

2. **Secondary Research**
   Purchase existing data from the marketplace. Secondary data is available through sources like academic journals, research databases, consulting firms, public libraries, schools, and government agencies.

3. **Anecdotal Evidence**
   If you can't afford to conduct research or buy existing data, your next best option is to rely on anecdotes. Talk to your subject matter experts. Talk to your sales reps. Your sales force is an untapped mine of persona intelligence. Talk to them to get an idea of what challenges customers and prospects are facing. Then, use their inputs to develop your personas. If gathering intelligence from Sales, here are some questions you should ask:

- What do people like the most about our product or service?
- What is their main objection to our solution?
- How soon are they looking to buy?
- What is their perception of our company?
- What problems are they seeking to solve?

How to Create Your Persona

As you get ready to craft the perfect embodiment of your ideal customer, you may find yourself drawing a blank. If this happens, don't freak out. Take three deep breaths through your nose and exhale through your mouth.

Ahhh.

Feel better?

Good.

Begin with a persona questionnaire.

Here are the five key attributes to include:

1. **Demographics**
   What's your persona's background? Do they skew male or female? Are they married or single? What's their age range? What's their annual income?

2. **Watering Holes**
   Where does your persona go to get information? Which TV shows, magazines, and websites do they frequent? Which social media groups do they belong to? Are they likely to get information from the local bar or industry trade shows?

3. **Action Drivers**
   What prompts your persona to take action?

4. **Doubts and Objections**

    What doubts and objections does your persona harbor? In other words, what is likely to prevent your persona from buying your product or service?

5. **Emotional Resonance**

    What emotional outcome is your persona seeking? Joy? Relief? Peace of mind?

The goal here is to get to know your prime audience as much as humanly possible. This requires a combination of data and creativity.

Now, imagine you've just met your persona at a bar. You're trying to get to know them—what they do for a living, what they do for fun, how they think, what they like or dislike, etc.

You want to learn everything you can about their goals, inclinations, sources of information, water cooler talking points, demographics, hobbies, etc. Even attributes that seem mundane can be helpful later in the persona building exercise. Don't worry about how to apply this information—we'll cover that later.

What's the Story?

Congratulations!

The intelligence gathering exercise is now over. Next, you're going to create your persona narratives.

Here's how:

- Using the information from the persona exercise, you will now create a brief story about your persona (no more than 1-2 paragraphs).

- The narrative should highlight your persona's influences, goals, and pain points. How is she moving through her buying journey? What is she learning about your company? How does it make her feel?

- Finally, you will wrap up your persona narrative with a value proposition that speaks to her biggest concerns and delivers a compelling solution.

What's in a Name?

We need a face to go along with the name. So, find an image that best resembles a real version of your persona. You can include highlights and business insights from the questionnaire, as well as any other useful information relevant to your industry.

Validate Your Persona

Review and vet the persona with your team. You want to make sure the persona looks, talks, and feels like a real customer. If done correctly, the persona, narrative and photo can fit neatly on one page, making it a handy reference for your marketing and sales teams.

Voila!

You have developed your primary persona—a realistic depiction of your ideal customer.

Encourage your marketing and sales team members to print and place a copy of your one-page persona somewhere visible. When your team is focused on meeting the needs of your ideal customers, your lead conversion will likely improve.

As Real as It Gets

Truly effective personas are more than just names and demographics. A persona is not a suit or skirt with a fancy title. Personas have real names plucked from real people. They have pets and pastimes; watering holes and sources of influence; goals and objectives; timelines and objections—attributes that help us visualize real people with real challenges.

Case Study: Personas in the Wild

When I worked as a content marketing manager at DMN3, we had a "war room" designated for persona development. It was a modest 8.5 x 10 room. Nothing fancy. We moved the desks to a corner and adorned the walls with giant post-its. My collaborator, Emily Mouton, and I would map out all the persona attributes on every sheet, then stand back and dramatize the personas. The exercise brought us closer to the mindset of our customers, yielding better content and more relevant leads.

We gave each persona distinct attributes that ranged from family life to hobbies. We labored over seemingly trivial details, such as their names and their day-to-day lives. We wanted to make sure we were describing real people with real challenges.

Our personas were senior-care candidates. We wanted to make sure we got the little details right. We interviewed people who had placed their loved ones in homes to better understand that process. We drew not just from our own experiences (because, remember—you are not your customer), but from those of others.

We pored over data to uncover the financial, psychological and physiological motivators behind the decision to put a family member in a nursing home. We were so specific that I still remember details of those personas and many others that I've created over the years. For instance, one of the personas was a 70-something year-old woman named Elizabeth. She lived alone because her eldest daughter lived 200 miles away. She owned seven cats.

The effort we put into developing personas paid off. We now had a clear understanding of our target audience whenever we created content. This helped us increase content quality and engagement. Our clients were blown away by the results.

But that was just the beginning.

Three months after the persona exercise, something interesting happened. I was assisting a crew with the delivery of free meals to the elderly. We visited six homes to deliver food to seniors who had no way of getting around during the holiday season. Most of them lived alone.

The effort was equally touching and rewarding. I was happy that we were able to make a difference in the lives of those men and women, even if it was just for a day. But, that's not why I'm telling you this story.

The third senior we served was a 70-ish woman who lived alone. Her only child lived nearly 200 miles away. I remember the commotion of trying to get through her gate because it was double-locked. Since she lived alone, she had to be sure it was secure.

When she finally let us in, I noticed she had seven cats running around everywhere. I remember wondering how she managed to take care of all those cats while also trying to take care of herself. Then it hit me: "Wow, I just met a real-life Elizabeth (our persona from the senior housing project)."

When you do the persona exercise correctly, your "fictitious" characters become as real as your audience—so real you might run into them someday.

Bonus

People change. And so do personas. Review your personas from time to time to make sure they're still accurate. You never know, your persona may have moved to the Bahamas.

BY MY SIDE

1. Create a persona questionnaire using the steps outlined in this chapter.
2. Develop a primary persona for your business based on the persona framework.
3. Write your persona narrative and buyer's journey.
4. Print your persona and place it somewhere visible (e.g. on your desk).
5. Consult your persona before creating your next content piece, whether it's an email or a social media post.

3

THE BUYER'S JOURNEY

"Always design a thing by considering it in its next larger context—a chair in a room, a room in a house, a house in an environment, an environment in a city plan."
Frank Lloyd Wright
(American architect, designer, writer, and educator)

I f you Google "face mask" you're going to get over 1.3 million search results. You don't have enough time to sort through 1.3 million search results to choose the best face mask. And neither does your customer.

There is no shortage of content. What's missing is not quality content. There's plenty of that on the Internet.

What's missing is content that speaks to the people you're trying to reach, right in their moment of need.

Google thrives in part due to this confluence of information deluge and scarcity of relevant content. Google has built its business model around sorting the web into buckets of relevant content, precisely validating the lack.

This is why a searcher would type in a term, browse the first five options, review two and click back out to Google.

Unless you're in the market for toilet paper, you might not take the first option presented. Even if you're shopping for T.P., you probably have a brand or texture preference. Soft or extra soft?

If your search isn't yielding success, you can click back out, try again, then check 10 more sites.

Two hours later, you're wondering how a simple search for "toilet paper" led you down the rabbit hole of George Carlin bits on YouTube.

That's how your customer feels. The good news is that you can do something about it.

Why is it so difficult to reach and convert the ideal customer who is already searching for your brand? What if there was a way to show up precisely in a customer's moment of need?

The key to showing up before the right customer is to first understand their buying journey. That's because content mapping and the buyer's journey go together like frat parties and beer cans.

Recall the definition of content mapping: *Content mapping is the strategic alignment of content with the needs of your customers throughout their buying journey.*

The Buyer's ARC

Awareness - Research - Conversion

Your Customer ——————→ Your Brand

The Buyer's Journey

The journey starts with a point of discovery. Then, it gradually progresses to research and serious consideration of the relevant options. Ultimately, your customer decides.

The goal is to close the gap between your brand and your customer's journey. To do this well, it helps to think like a buyer. For example, think back to the last time you bought something important.

- What events or actions triggered the thought to either research or buy that thing?
- Did you buy it out of boredom, routine, or necessity?
- Was it a small purchase, like mint, or a big-ticket item like a couch?
- What did you do when you first thought about buying it?
- Was it an impulse buy?
- Did you evaluate a few options online?
- Did you look up reviews of the product? Did you ask friends or family for advice?
- What did you do next?
- And after that?

This is your buyer's journey.

Now, do the same exercise for your customer.

Think of your primary persona and write down their answers to the above questions. This should give you a picture of their buying journey.

The buyer's journey is not a vanity exercise. Pay attention to how your customers are moving through the buying process. Are they hasty buyers placing today's orders for yesterday's delivery? Or, are they more structured and comprehensive in their buying process?

With this knowledge, you can begin to map content to the different stages, needs and timeline of your customers. When you prioritize the information needs of your customers, you increase your chance of generating a lead or a sale.

But, don't just take it from me. According to the 2019 Content Marketing Institute report, 77% of the most successful marketers develop content based on specific points/stages in the buyer's journey and 81% prioritize delivering the right content to the right audience(s) at optimal times (*aka those who map content to the buyer's journey*)–compared to 28% and 32% of the least successful marketers, respectively. The difference is remarkable.

The Sweet Spot

The key to developing an effective content map is to identify your *sweet spot*. This is where your solution meets your persona's pain points. It's precisely why you want to close with your elevator pitch next to your persona's pain points

One of the primary objectives of the buyer's journey is to help clarify what matters to your customers, so you can meet them at the point of need. Going through the buyer's journey exercise forces you to think about where your solution meets your persona's pain points.

Stages of the Buyer's Journey

There are many iterations of the buyer's journey, but we'll focus on the three primary stages.

The three primary stages are:
- Awareness
- Research, and
- Conversion

This is a simplified version of the process. If you sell a more complicated product, you can add more stages to the process.

The buyer's journey starts with an expression of symptoms of an underlying problem (*awareness*). The prospect then assigns a specific name to the problem and starts reviewing a few options (*research & consideration*). Finally, your prospect defines a solution, strategy or approach (*conversion*).

To help you remember the buyer's journey, think of the trajectory as an ARC: Awareness, Research and Conversion.

Content Mapping...Hollywood Style

A typical movie has a three-arc story structure:
I. the setup
II. the conflict
III. the resolution

Content marketing is a form of storytelling. And, the filmmaker's storytelling structure is a useful way to think about content mapping.

The setup is the trigger—the moment of awareness and initial step toward a solution. Conflict is the research phase, when a buyer is still weighing different options. The resolution is the finality of the buying process, during which a customer opts for a course of action.

If we reimagine the movie storytelling formula as a content mapping process, it looks like this:

Movies	Content Marketing
The setup	The trigger / awareness
The conflict	The research
The resolution	The conversion

As people express different needs at different stages of their buying process, they also expect different solutions. According to a Pardot State of Demand Generation report, 76% of buyers prefer different content at each stage of their research.

Different buyers require different messages. A customer who is merely browsing solutions is not necessarily ready to have a discount shoved in her face. Conversely, if she has already made up her mind to buy, then a discount could help speed up the process.

Your content map should identify the relevant content to help solve problems for your buyer as she moves through the process. This helps nudge buyers along, while delivering real solutions.

Consider how you might go about buying a car, for example. You'll probably start by identifying what you really need (awareness); You might look up resources and reviews online to further educate yourself (research & consideration) before deciding on a short list of options and ultimately making a choice (conversion).

Let's consider the buyer's ARC in this scenario, but this time with the content mapped to each stage of the journey:

Awareness

Customer Scenario: "I need to buy a car. Just not sure which."

Brand Content: "The 10 Highest Rated Cars to Buy Right Now" (Blog Post)

Research

Customer Scenario: "I'm considering a long list of car brands within my price range. I'm looking at safety reviews and trying to decide on a short list of brands."

Brand Content: The 5 Safest Cars of the Year (Safety Report, Blog Post, eBook)

Conversion

Customer Scenario: "I've narrowed the list of cars, and I'm ready to go test-drive a few to find the right match.

Brand Content: Shop all cars. Get 30-day money back. No questions asked. (Offer)

Not everyone's journey is as linear as what is outlined here. Some will hop from awareness to conversion, or from research to conversion. (More on unconventional buying journeys later.) Still, these three stages largely capture the path most customers typically travel, from discovery to purchase.

ONCE UPON A TIME...

1. Develop a one-page narrative describing your persona's buying journey based on data and anecdotes.
2. Validate it with your sales team and customer experience staff, if you have one, to make sure it accurately captures the buyer's journey.

4

CONTENT STRATEGY

*"We join spokes together in a wheel, but it is the
center hole that makes the wagon move."*
Lao Tzu
(Chinese philosopher and author of *Tao Te Ching*)

Every year, the Content Marketing Institute surveys marketers to understand their strategies, challenges and opportunities. Every year, the leading cause of content marketing disconnect seems to be the same: the lack of a *documented* content strategy. Note the choice of words: *a documented content strategy*. It's not enough to have a strategy in your head or on your napkin; It must be documented. Like a map, it's only useful if it's visible to the people trying to navigate the landscape.

Elements of Content Strategy

Your content strategy should include the following seven elements:

1. Your marketing objectives
2. Your personas

3. Your customer journeys
4. Your value propositions
5. Your content themes and topics
6. Your content maps
7. Your success metrics

Delivery Channels

Like manufactured goods, your content needs a delivery system. Content calls for unique distribution, depending on your goals.

Let's look at a few delivery channels.

Website

Back in the olden days, your sales force was your primary source of leads and sales. If Sales made no call, you made no sale. Today, your website is your key salesperson. A website designed with customers in mind can keep bringing in leads and sales while you sleep. Literally.

I'm not saying that your website is a "Set it and forget it" platform. It's not. You need to do the work necessary to make it produce results. And doing this correctly makes it easier to attract the right customers.

Another way to think of your website is as your online storefront. If you had a brick and mortar store that sold furniture, how would you organize your products? If I walked into your furniture store, would I find that bedroom pieces are separated from the living room selection? Consider organizing your website the same way you would organize your physical store. The medium is different, but your customers still expect some sort of order that makes shopping a breeze.

Here are the four main types of content you should highlight on your website:

- Your products and services sequenced in order of value to your customers
- Educational resources, such as blog posts, articles and research findings
- Interactive tools that help customers solve problems
- Credibility signals, such as customer reviews, testimonials, and awards

Email

The email inbox is one of the most competitive marketing environments. Despite the growing competition, email remains a highly effective direct marketing channel. The reason email still works has little to do with how well marketers can craft emails. Email works because email is essential.

Consider how email differs from other channels. If you want to promote your small business on social media, you have several options to choose from: Facebook, Instagram, LinkedIn, Twitter, Tiktok, Clubhouse and on and on. But if you wanted to promote your small business using email, well, you only have one option: email.

Likewise, people like checking their email with high frequency. There's simply no substitute for email.

Avoid treating your customers as an email database that *must* be optimized. A better approach is to see the people on your email list for who they are—*real people* with *real scenarios*. When you see it from this light, then you can begin to help them solve problems. Solving problems is what builds lasting relationships.

Here are just a few examples of how to maximize email as a distribution channel:

- Personalize content by intent and scenario
- Engage in one-to-one conversations
- Get to know your customers better
- Launch new initiatives
- Promote educational blog posts and articles
- Increase customer loyalty
- Win back lapsed customers

The good news is you don't have to compromise cost to use email effectively. Email is the least expensive means of winning new customers.

Consider this Cost per Acquisition breakdown by *eMarketer*:

- Direct Mail - $27.35
- Social Media - $21.95
- Paid Search - $21.50
- Online Display - $19.50
- Email - $10.23

It gets better. Email generally produces more long-term customers than social media. This is because people still prefer the personable touch of email. Smart marketers use email to extend conversations with customers. You can personalize your tone and message, all the way down to a recipient's first name, nickname and birthday.

When using email to promote your content, keep these best practices in mind:

- Send your emails from a person instead of a brand
- Be consistent with your send format
- A/B test one thing at a time (e.g. subject line or call-to-action)
- Communicate clearly and in a conversational tone
- Address your email reader as an individual—not as a group (e.g. "You," not "All of you")
- Make it worth the reader's time
- Map your email to the recipient's stage in the buyer's journey (i.e. awareness, research, consideration)

Social Media

I still remember when social media entered the marketing building around the mid-2000s. Everything changed. Before social media, brands controlled the narrative. It was a one-way conversation. Social media levelled the playing field, giving customers permission to talk back.

Today, customers have a voice, and social media is their megaphone. They use social channels to brag about positive experiences or complain about bad ones. Which experience will your brand seek to create?

Companies that continue to play by the old rule of one-way conversations struggle on social media. The best brands engage. They activate the tribal power of social networks to increase reach and resonance.

Above all, social media is a great way to listen to customers and identify opportunities for innovation and improvement. The best social media pages listen, engage, and delight. They seek to put the *social* back in *social media*.

Paid Search

Search is a simple way for a customer to raise her hand and say, "I have a problem." The goal of your paid search campaign is to tell that customer that you have the solution to her problem. This makes paid search one of the most effective channels of distribution, especially for customers at the bottom of the funnel.

Google runs the largest, most profitable advertising platform, AdWords. It's an online auction of ads, where you can bid on potential customers who have indicated a problem. Just because it's cheap doesn't mean it's always the right channel for every marketing scenario.

When using paid media, consider the following:
- Who are you trying to reach?
- What problem are they trying to solve?
- How relevant is your landing page to their search query?
- How will you measure the success of your ads?

Print

Though often declared dead, print is still alive and kicking. Print materials, such as brochures, flyers and banners are ideal for in-person events. Print is still the primary mode of communication for many industries and older demographics.

Think of your print assets as a spoke on the hub of your content program. Use print to drive traffic to your conversion page, which is likely to live on your website.

Once you have clarity on what you want to say and who you need to say it to, simply adapt your message to your print materials. This makes it easier for your sales team to stay on brand and on message. Start with the digital assets, and then repurpose them for print.

Examples of print materials:
- Your company's capabilities overview brochure
- Data sheets and FAQ handouts
- Customer-centric flyers, mapped to intent and scenario
- Business cards
- Coupons

Content Purpose

Random acts of marketing rarely yield repeatable results. Every piece of content you create should be designed with a purpose in mind. Strategically, your content should serve one of the following five (5) purposes:

1. **Shareability**: This type of content can be a great link-building asset. Shareable content can be widgets, interactive tools or viral posts.
2. **Education**: Educational content provides valuable information to the customer, helping them make

an informed buying decision. If done correctly, this type of content has the added value of positioning your brand as an authority on the subject.

3. **Entertainment**: This content should aim to entertain and captivate. It's there to mix things up a bit.

4. **Conversion**: Quality content that converts plays at the intersection of your elevator pitch and the pain points of your prospective clients.

5. **Conversation**: This type of content primarily exists to promote conversations around your brand, products, and service.

If some of the categories overlap, that's normal. For instance, the same content could be entertaining and shareable. Don't sweat the overlap. The purpose of the categorization is to help you avoid vague content and approach content creation in a more strategic manner.

Meet Your Customers Where They Are

You wouldn't build a house and *then* decide how many occupants it should hold. So, your content strategy should not be forced to fit channels and technology. It should be intuitive and sequential.

Start with your personas. Then, design your marketing blueprint around their buying journey. Meet your customers where they are, and you'll have a better chance of resonating.

THE BLUEPRINT

Create a content strategy for your business and include the following:

- Your marketing objectives
- Your personas
- Your customer's buying journey
- Your value propositions
- Your content channels
- Your content themes and topics
- Your content maps

5

THE CONTENT MAP

"My mother, you know, I want her to like it, but she's not exactly my target audience."
John Legend
(Grammy-winning artist; NME Interview, Nov 20, 2006)

I f it's alright with you, we'll start with a short exercise. Try to visualize your ideal customer. I'm not talking about names on a spreadsheet. Rather, I'm talking about a real person. Surely, an image comes to mind. Got it?

Great.

Now, imagine that your ideal customer is going through life on autopilot. She wakes up at 6:30 am every day. Bathroom. Breakfast. Driveway. Work.

At some point during the day, she comes in contact with your content, perhaps while browsing social media during her lunch break. What is your persona's first interaction with your brand?

The marketer seeks to present content that speaks directly to the right persona at the right time. Content and context go hand in hand.

Consider the issues that would matter to *you* in each stage of *your* buying journey, if you were a customer thinking about picking up your product. The information you'll need when you first become aware of a problem is different from what you need when you're ready to buy.

For example, you likely start out with little information about a new product. After all, you've never bought it before. But by the time you're ready to buy, you tend to have significantly more knowledge and confidence based on your research.

Present the right content at the right moment. If you don't have enough content, don't worry about this right now. We'll get to work on how to develop a content library later. For now, we'll assume you have all the content you need (*Spoiler Alert: You probably do*). Focus on mapping your content to the buying stages (i.e. awareness, research and conversion).

Awareness

A buyer in the awareness stage is experiencing a problem and needs help understanding, researching and identifying solutions.

At this stage, your prospects are not yet ready to commit to a solution. They are merely trying to identify a solution to their problem. Heck, they might not even have a name for this problem. They simply know that one exists.

Here, your focus should be to educate and engage. Use content to drive traffic to your website and convert visitors to leads. This allows you to continue the education process.

In terms of format, think light, bite-sized informative content. The goal is to use less intrusive methods that warm up visitors and establish a relationship. Earn their permission so you can continue the conversation.

Earnest marketers make the mistake of trying to force a sale at the awareness level. This will likely fracture trust and end the conversation abruptly. Instead, focus on providing value and helping people make informed decisions on their own.

Here are the types of content that will appeal to buyers in the awareness phase:

- Blog posts
- eBooks
- Webinars
- Social media posts

PLAN OF ATTACK

» Create an editorial calendar to help you blog consistently
» Define a cadence (e.g., 1-3 times a week)
» Create a sales and marketing dashboard to track results
» Promote your blog posts through email

Research

A buyer in the research stage has identified a problem and is now considering possible solutions.

At this stage, your prospects know a bit about your business, but they still have questions. What sets you apart from your competitors? Why should people buy from you? This is the point where shoppers start whittling down their options. They're evaluating vendors, and they're close to making up their minds. Use longer form content offers like eBooks and in-depth case studies to demonstrate your value and seal the deal.

Here are the types of content that will appeal to buyers in the research phase:

- In-depth eBooks
- White papers
- Advanced webinars
- Case studies
- Customer testimonials
- Educational videos
- Industry reports
- Data sheets
- Demo videos

SHOW & PROVE

» Compile a list of credibility signals for your business (e.g. testimonials, awards, case studies and fact sheets)

» Create a case study with your primary persona in mind

» Promote your case studies to your prospects via email

Conversion

A buyer in the conversion stage has selected a specific list of companies and is mulling further engagement.

These prospects are well informed. They know what they want, and they're ready to take the next step. Reserve your best offers for conversion-level prospects: free trials, evaluations, and demos.

You spend a lot of time on lead generation and content marketing, but if those efforts aren't properly aligned, your investment will not yield results. To be effective, your offers should make the benefits clear to the customer and speak to their immediate needs.

Here are the types of content that will appeal to buyers in the conversion phase:

- Free consultation
- Calculators
- Free trials
- Coupons
- Analyst reports
- Live demos

CONVERSION POINTS

» Write an eBook addressing an urgent question on your persona's mind

» Add conversion paths (e.g. *Contact Us* forms) to every page on your website

» Host a webinar to engage prospects and directly answer their questions

A Content Map Illustrated

So, you're probably asking, "Henry, how do I know where my customers are in their buying journey?" It's a great question. And it's one of the most difficult questions in content marketing. To answer this question, we need to develop a big picture understanding of what customers know about their situation, as well as what they've signaled to us based on intent and scenario.

For example, if a customer with back pain is in the market for a new mattress, his awareness-stage inquiry might not even include the word "mattress." Perhaps, this customer isn't even aware that his bed is a key contributor to back pain. Likely, his initial search might include terms such as "how to get rid of back pain." This is a great opportunity to educate the customer through well-researched articles showing the link between back pain and sleep quality.

To further illustrate, let's take a look at what your content map would look like, using the mattress shopper example. Pay attention to the customer's needs and how they align with different offers and channels.

Your content map is a piece of your overall content strategy. It should look like a table with four columns and five rows. The columns represent the scenarios, along with the three main stages of the buyer's journey (awareness, research and conversion). The rows represent intent, channel, purpose, and success metrics.

Scenario	Awareness	Research	Conversion
Intent	I want to get rid of back pain and I'm not sure if a new mattress will make a difference.	I've identified the 3 attributes of a quality mattress, and I have a list of brands to pick from.	I'm finally ready to start comparing brands. I'll test a few mattresses before making my final decision.
Channel	Blog, Social media; Infographics	White papers, case studies; customer reviews	Demos, Customer testimonials
Purpose	Increase awareness; Subscription sign-ups	Lead acquisition; Lead nurturing	Customer acquisition
Metrics	Newsletter sign-ups; Social media engagement; Blog engagement	Email click-thru rate; Landing page conversion	Close rate

If you look at this example closely, you can see the progression of the customer's knowledge. At the *awareness* level, there's still some fuzziness ("Do I need a new mattress or some other back pain remedy?") With the help of a few well-researched articles, he narrows it down to mattresses and starts considering specific brands in the *research* phase. By the time we arrive at the *conversion* stage, the customer now has clarity on the issue and is ready to act.

If you've set up your content map correctly, you've accompanied the customer on this journey. You provided valuable information and helped him make an informed decision. When he's ready to buy, who do you think he's likely to call?

Your Content Map Tells a Story

Remember the 3-arc storytelling technique we discussed earlier? You'll recall that it started with a setup. Next came the conflict. Finally, there was a resolution. You can now see how a content map does the same thing: it tells a story in a similar trajectory.

Continuing with the mattress shopper example, consider how storytelling helps create a content map.

John wants to buy a mattress (the setup). He has chronic back pain and is unsure which brand to trust (the conflict). Luckily, Unicorn Mattress offers a specialty brand of mattress with a higher number of coils and thicker padding, providing ample back and spine support for John (the resolution).

Knowing what we now know about John and his back pain (based on his search query, for example), Unicorn Mattress can then map content to the various stages of his buying journey.

How exactly would they go about doing that?

In the awareness stage, John is concerned about choosing the right mattress for back support. Unicorn Mattress decides to push blog posts and social media content addressing the issue (e.g. "How to Choose the Perfect Mattress for Back Support" or "The Best Mattress Brands for Back Pain").

In the research and consideration phase, the brand would showcase customer reviews and success stories of real customers just like John who are now enjoying their best sleep ever, despite years of chronic back pain.

Finally, for its conversion-phase content, Unicorn Mattress would provide a call to action inviting John to stop by a store and lie on the mattress he's been researching. This offer requires more commitment, so it is mostly likely to resonate only after John has researched his options and is now ready to take the next step. At the very minimum, he has whittled down his options one last time. When he makes that trip to the store, he is a very warm lead and will likely make a purchase. John gets the mattress of his dreams. Unicorn Mattress makes a sale. Everyone wins.

This example is the opposite of the spray and pray approach of traditional content marketing. The idea is that you simply spray everyone with the same content and pray someone bites. This is type of "Hail Mary" content is too generic to be meaningful.

The alternative is to present relevant, context-rich content to the right person at the right time. Start with the resolution in mind and work backwards through the conflict and setup.

Unconventional Customer Journeys

So far, we've learned that people think differently throughout the buying cycle. There is one exception to this rule: customers who leap from the point of discovery to the conversion stage of the journey. These customers don't necessarily go through the conventional ARC (awareness, research, and conversion).

Some buyers start out right in the middle of the cycle. They may jump to the conversion phase, if they already have some idea of what they want coming into the process. Analyze your audience and pay attention to unconventional buyers, so you can map content accordingly.

For these buyers, don't try to force them through a more systematic buying process. Initiate contact as soon as possible. If they're ready to buy immediately, you have the best chance of reaching them by responding to their inquiries in a timely fashion.

Context is key when mapping content for all your audiences, but this is especially true for unconventional customers.

When I worked as a content director at a marketing agency, our team once grappled with how to create lead generation content for an unconventional customer. We were developing content strategy for a law firm, and we felt stuck for a moment. I asked our copywriter, Alan Spackman, if we'd considered mapping content to the different customer lifecycle stages.

"For this client," Alan responded, "the consideration stage is in the back of the cop car."

We discussed it further and Alan swiftly came up with a solution. He suggested it would be more effective to build enough resonance and awareness so that the persona was predisposed to the client by the time the need arrived. Always keep the customer's scenario in mind when mapping your content.

Here are some unconventional scenarios to consider.
- Awareness → Conversion
- Research → Conversion
- Advocacy → Conversion

The Gospel According to Brand Advocates

If a customer is thrilled with your brand, she will come back over and over. She'll buy from you frequently and tell others about your company. This customer is your *brand advocate*. Your ambassador. Your very own evangelist, ready to spread the gospel of your brand. Let the church say, "Amen."

Brand advocates influence others by publicizing your brand on social media, writing product reviews and sharing their experiences with friends and family.

Your brand advocates are an asset to your marketing. Don't take them for granted. Continue to feed them quality, personalized content. Encourage them to share positive experiences with their network.

Focus on content that makes your advocates proud to support your brand. Every now and then, throw in a loyalty-based offer to sweeten the relationship. Reassure them that they've made a great choice by not changing the channel.

THE ROADMAP

1. Review the primary persona you created earlier
2. List your persona's questions as s/he moves through the buying journey
3. Create a content map for your persona using the Unicorn Mattress template

6

B2B CONTENT MAPPING

*"In the world of ideas, to name something is to own it.
If you can name an issue, you can own the issue."*
Thomas L. Friedman
(Author and three-time Pulitzer Prize winner)

Everything we have discussed throughout this book—personas, buyer's journey, content strategy—are all relevant to business-to-business customers. B2B customers should be represented by well-informed personas, defined according to their stages in the buying process and aligned with content strategy.

After all, businesses sell to humans. And, whether you're selling to consumers or businesses, the objective is the same: to earn and retain a customer.

That said, it's true that B2B marketing has some unique attributes that should be considered within the context of content architecture.

A Family That Buys Together

First, the bad news. B2B companies typically make buying decisions as a group. Did you know that the more decision makers are involved in the buying process the lower the likelihood of a purchase? According to a study by CEB, if a group of 5 or more people are involved, the probability of a purchase is much lower.

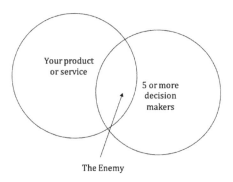

The good news is it doesn't have to be this way. The obvious solution is to figure out who matters the most and focus on reaching him or her. Also, consider mapping content to every key decision maker. This requires a bit of leg work. For example, if you're planning to send a gift in the mail to try and get a meeting, send the same gift and letter to all five decision makers. It will provide them with fodder for conversation when they run into one another in the break room. This jumpstarts the conversation, bringing them closer to the same page.

Steady Wins the Race

Pinched by fierce competition, it's easy for B2B marketers   to succumb to the trap of hasty marketing. When mapping content to B2B buyers, however, keep in mind that you will be dealing with a more complex buying environment. Longer buying cycles are common. Be patient and plan accordingly. Consistency is your friend.

Defeating the Status Quo

When selling to B2B personas, your enemy is not the competition; your enemy is the status quo. Your inability to make a sale has nothing to do with your product. It has everything to do with those interested in protecting the status quo.

Sure, Brad recognizes the benefits of your software, including the potential cost savings. You've only explained it to him 15 times. Your charts are beautiful, and the cost savings estimator is precise, interactive, and clear. But Brad doesn't want change, because it involves risking his social capital within the company. So, Brad keeps on trucking along while the company continues to mire in mediocrity.

What can you do?

First, find out which of the decision makers is only looking out for self and who is looking out for the company. Make sure they have enough authority to pull the trigger. Then, focus your efforts on empowering them as advocates for the solution. Challenge your customer to see the bigger picture. Incidentally, they become the hero.

Mapping Content to B2B Buyer Personas

Once you get a clear picture of the decision makers, map your content according to their interests. The group will consist of different roles and professional backgrounds.

For example, consider a group made up of the following personas and note how the content could be mapped to the right appeal.

Persona's Job Title	Responsibility	Interests	Ideal Content
Procurement Director	Product acquisition; Product evaluation	Numbers; Cost savings; Quality & reputation	ROI calculators; Data sheets; Case studies with measurable benefits
Project Manager	Team management; Process co-ordination	Team efficiency; Product effectiveness; Safety and protocol	Demo or in-depth presentation; Safety fact sheets; Peer reviews; Customer testimonials
Engineer	Designs and specifies the product; Evaluates products for quality & specification accuracy	Product quality Prioritizes safety and reliability	Specification sheet; Comprehensive information page on the product; Testimonials from fellow engineers

In each case, you can see how the priorities are aligned with the roles and responsibilities. So, the content, channels and offers should match your persona's intent and scenario.

Trust and Credibility

Trust is essential when dealing with customers. But we can't build trust by constantly poking our content at people until they flinch. Instead, we must concentrate on content that will appeal to the right people and show value.

People recognize when there is thought behind a prospecting approach. Business decision makers value the little things, like not demanding an hour of their time. Thirty minutes of concise and focused pitching shows that you did the research upfront. More importantly, it shows that you respect their time.

HOMEWORK

Personas require research, not guesswork. Invest the time upfront to understand who you will be selling to, so you can design the content map that best resonates with them.

7

CONTENT LIBRARY

"Don't just create content to get credit for being clever—create content that will be helpful, insightful, or interesting for your target audience."
David Ogilvy
("The Father of Advertising")

Have you ever read an article or watched a video and thought to yourself, "Yes! That's me." Perhaps, you even hollered those words so loudly that your neighbors dropped in to check on you. Okay, maybe I'm describing myself here, but you get the point. Great content singles you out like someone being paged in a crowded hotel lobby.

It's no accident that some content speak to us, while others don't. Architects of relevant content have a near-psychic understanding of their personas. More importantly, they also understand where you are in your buying journey and what content is most likely to speak to you.

By the end of this book, you'll be able to create that same "Yes! That's me" effect with your content. You're already half-way there. Let's recap.

First, you identified your personas. Then, you defined your buyer's journey. Finally, you developed and documented your content strategy. Now comes the fun part. It's time to build a world-class content library. You don't have to create everything from scratch. You can start by repurposing existing content.

The Content Audit

Whether you have a full library of content or a library of zero, you have more content under your nose than you realize. We will uncover your hidden content shortly. The question is not whether you have enough content; the question is, "Do you have the *right* content for the people you're trying to reach?"

There is one way to find out—take stock of your content library. Audit your content to find the gaps that need to be plugged.

Where to Find Hidden Content

If you have articles, blog posts, and white papers, that's great. Below are a few additional sources of content.

- Your website
- Customer testimonials
- Social media reviews
- Google My Business reviews
- Case studies
- Datasheets

If you have these, you definitely have content that could be harnessed. You probably don't think of Google reviews as part of your content library. Yet, customer reviews can be repurposed as social media posts, helping boost your credibility.

Factors to Consider When Auditing Your Content

- **Persona**: Identify the proper audience. You probably have multiple personas (primary, secondary, influencer). Be sure to note the appropriate persona for each content asset. If it's not clear who the content is for, consider revamping it with a relevant persona in mind.
- **Lifecycle stage**: Where is your persona in the lifecycle stage? An ideal content audit identifies the prospect's lifecycle stage (e.g. prospect, lead, marketing-qualified lead, sales-qualified lead, customer, evangelist, etc.)
- **Ready status**: Is the content ready to be used in your marketing program? Is it time-sensitive? Is it evergreen? If it's not ready for immediate use, identify what it would take to move it into the "ready" status, such as a quick, creative touch-up or updated copy.
- **Topic**: What is the topic of the content piece? Is this relevant to your persona?
- **Format**: What is the current format of the content? Does the format still work? Maybe you have an old case study that would work better as a blog post.
- **Purpose:** Why was the content developed? Examples of content purpose include shareability, edu-

cation, entertainment, conversion, or conversation. Does the original purpose still stand? Could it be revised to fit a better purpose?

- **Customer journey**: Your personas have unique concerns, depending on where they are in their journey. Identify where your content is best used in the customer journey. For example, if it's a comprehensive eBook that creates awareness around a problem, then this is likely an awareness-stage content. If it's a case study that shares a story about how your brand helped solve a problem, it's probably a research-phase asset.

How to Organize Your Content Inventory

As a former content director, I understand the pain of trying to wade through unstructured folders of content. To ease the process, I developed an organizing system that shows me all available content in one convenient view.

This system tracks seven key content attributes, including the topic, format, persona, lifecycle stage, customer journey, location and notes related to the status of the content.

Using this template, you'll quickly spot gaps in your content inventory and work towards filling them. Include as much or as little detail as you need.

Content Auditing Template

Topic	Format (Type)	Location	Persona	Lifecycle Stage	Customer Journey	Purpose	Notes
How to Find a Unicorn	Article	Website	Primary	Prospect	Awareness	Educate	Outdated stats; Update

As you audit your content library, you'll uncover ideas for new material. This is good news because you're ready to develop better content.

The 3 Essential Content Categories

To make sure content has a VIP seat at the marketing table, you need the right messages aligned with the right persona.

You need a balanced mix of the following three content categories:

1. *Original Content*: Content you create from scratch
2. *Curated Content*: Content curated from trusted, vetted industry sources
3. *Premium Content*: Engagement accelerator content, such as case studies, videos and webinars

How to Source New Content Ideas

You've completed your content audit. You've identified what gaps need to be closed. Now, it's time to roll up your sleeves and get to work creating engaging content for your marketing program.

Here are some ideas of where to turn for topics relevant to your audience:

1. **Go where your personas congregate**

   How do you identify the topics your audience cares about? You could ask the marketplace, take a risk and just experiment, or you could check to see if people are already questioning.

   If there's a trade association or publication that caters to your audience, chances are you have something worth exploring. This is one of the best ways I've found to source topics.

   As part of your audience research, you will need to understand consumption habits and information sources. What podcasts do they listen to? What webinars and trade shows do they frequent? What websites and social networks do they visit? Go where your personas congregate and you'll learn a great deal about their concerns.

2. **Set up a social listening studio**

   As marketers, we tend to focus on our own noise. We need to stop, look and listen. When we listen—via social media posts and search queries—we learn a lot about the real issues that face our real personas. You have many sensors available today, including Google Alerts, review monitoring sites, and social media. Once you've listened, it becomes easier to respond with useful content.

3. **Survey your audience**

   A simple survey asking your target audience about their biggest challenges can yield amazing insights. You can do this by using any of the survey platforms out there. If you're running progressive profiling on your landing pages, this is another way to self-generate data. Pay attention to the patterns of responses and user behavior.

4. **Turn user questions into topics**

   One of the most underrated topic research tools is the Site Search feature. Go under the hood. Review Site Search patterns to see what your site visitors are researching. This could yield valuable topics and inform strategies that directly meet the needs of your customers and prospective customers.

5. **Interview thought leaders**

   Interview an expert that caters to the audience you wish to reach. If you sell jewelry, sit down with a fashion blogger to check the pulse of the industry. A 30-minute interview could yield months of material for your content library. If you can't find time to sit down with experts, use a service, such as HARO, to solicit input from professionals in your space. Ask them where they think the industry is headed, and you'll be amazed at how much you'll learn.

6. **Tap internal subject matter specialists**

   You don't have to travel too far to find experts. A subject matter expert could be lurking right in your backyard. If you work at a small company, you probably know your experts. If you work at a large organization, ask a more experienced colleague or creep around on LinkedIn to seek out your internal experts.

7. **Ask Google**

    Use keyword research to determine relevant topics for blog posts and content offers. Keyword-based content offers two primary benefits:

    1. Your content is pre-optimized—your personas are already looking up these topics

    2. Your content has a higher chance of resonating, given that it is directly addressing a known need.

    Keyword analysis is one of your safest bets for finding relevant topics.

8. **Add a new slant to a familiar topic**

    Let's face it, very few people have the time, brain power, and ingenuity to constantly generate entirely new ideas. You can keep your content machine running by rethinking existing assets. Think back to your audit template and look for content that could be easily repurposed. Remember, your primary goal is not to develop award-winning content; it's to serve your customers and get feedback.

9. **Syndicate research materials**

    If you have the ideas and resources, consider creating your own research. If this isn't feasible, the next best option is to have your best copywriter summarize existing research findings, so they are available in one place. Be sure to cite properly. Provide sources so your readers can explore the topics in depth.

How to Create Remarkable Content

Once you've figured out what you want to say and to whom, the challenge is to create truly remarkable content. You may choose to create your marketing content in-house or outsource to a freelancer. In either case, here are the qualities to strive for with your content.

1. **Show, don't tell**

   As a journalist, editors always advised me to "show, don't tell." What exactly do editors mean when they tell us to show, not tell? It's about treating your content like an experience. Rather than a bunch of words or video clips, your content should take the audience by her hand and guide her through the experience, sequence by sequence. The idea is that we focus on showing a story, rather than blandly stating facts.

2. **Don't generalize. Personalize**

   Content mapping is the opposite of mass marketing. It's the new engagement model. Mapping content to intent and scenario is the key to building trust and engagement. Yet, so many companies forget the lesson of the new engagement model. The new engagement model is more specific. It's a conversation between two people. It's not B2B or B2C.

It's H2H. Human to human.

Marketing that speaks to people one-to-one is more likely to resonate than marketing that speaks to everyone, or one-to-many. One-to-one says to your audience, "You're not just a number." It says, "I see you."

3. **Consider intent and scenario**

   Great content is not all things to all people. It not only speaks to a specific person; it also fulfills a set purpose. The purpose could be to spread awareness, influence a thought process, or help someone navigate a problem.

SHOWTIME

1. Think of a website where your persona is likely to go for information.
2. Note the 5 most important questions or topics on the website.
3. Write a blog post addressing one of the questions.
4. Remember: Show, don't tell.

8

CHANNEL MAPPING

"You cannot expect to catch a trout by shouting at it from the riverbank proclaiming that you're a great fisherman. You need a hook with feathers on it."
Melchior Incza
(Walter Slezak's character in the 1945 film Cornered)

O K...so your company makes the best unicorn sleeveless jacket. It begs the question: How do we get this in front of people who want unicorn sleeveless jackets? The trick is to choose the right channels for your content. It's not a coincidence. It's a strategy.

You've heard the saying, "It's not just what you say; it's how you say it." I like to think of marketing channels as the valuable exterior to the indispensable interior of content marketing. Channels matter. The type of content that resonates on social media, for example, might not necessarily be the ideal content for an email campaign.

As you develop your content strategy, consider the best way to deliver each piece of content. For example, awareness-stage content is best delivered through social media and blog posts; research-stage content works great through email; and conversion-stage content is best delivered through direct communication, such as phone conversations.

Yet, these are rules-of-thumb to help you get started. Don't limit yourself by channel. Instead, leave your campaign open to the possibility of breaking a rule or two. After all, marketing is part-art, part-experimentation.

Content Mapping by Channel

By now, you already know that your buyer's journey should simulate the path traveled by your persona. We also discussed how people need different types of content to help them make informed decisions. It's just as important to deliver the content through the right channel. The process will vary, depending on the channel you choose.

To illustrate, here is a breakdown of the relationship between the buyer's journey and channel strategy.

Buyer's Journey	Awareness	Research	Conversion
Channel	Social media posts; Blog posts Email; Infographics; Consumer guides; Ebooks	Blog posts; Email Webinars; Case Studies; White papers; Pricing page;	Demos; Free trial Free consultation; Price calculators

Content Mapping and Your Marketing Channels

Let's take a closer look at the relationship between your content map and your marketing channels.

Website

Your website is the central unit of your marketing ecosystem. It's also an essential marketing tool for brand advocates. People typically refer others to the website of their favorite brands, so make sure yours is worth its weight in bragging rights.

Channel	Awareness	Research	Conversion
Website	Great for sharing informative content	Great for blogs, resources and customer testimonials	Ideal for landing pages inviting customers to request a quote

Email Marketing

In the early days of social media marketing, some predicted the demise of email. Those people have egg on their faces now, because email is still alive and kicking. Today, email marketing remains a valuable asset for driving conversions.

Channel	Awareness	Research	Conversion	Advocacy
Email	Promote educational resources like blog posts and case studies	Deliver relevant advice and testimonials to boost credibility	Drive customers to a landing page; Reactivate lapsed customers; Follow up with those who forgot to check out	Nurture existing clients; Promote loyalty program

Social Media

Social media is the great megaphone, and it can be useful throughout the buying journey. Here are some ideal scenarios to unlock the power of social media.

Channel	Awareness	Research	Conversion	Advocacy
Social Media	Educate, enlighten and engage new customers and prospects; Increase brand awareness; Show off your brand personality	Promote offers to generate leads	Drive conversions by pushing traffic to a landing page	Encourage brand evangelists to share positive experiences; Promote customer testimonials

Search

Many of us turn to Google when we have a question about a problem. It helps to know what keywords and query terms people use to look you up online. Conduct keyword research using the Google Keyword Planner, so you can mimic the language of your prospects.

The depth of your content and the choice of words should reflect their interest level, brand predisposition, language and subject matter competence.

Awareness
- Respond to customer inquiries
- Build awareness with new customers

Research
- Share credibility signals, such as testimonials and relevant awards
- Showcase comparison charts, case studies and interactive widgets
- Share consumer guides, eBooks, white papers, fact sheets, etc.

Conversion
- Generate leads through conversion landing pages

Key Takeaways

1. **Consider Your Customer's Intent**

   Intent is the purpose behind your customer's actions. When it comes to mapping out your content strategy, nothing is more critical to success than understanding what your personas are up to and why. Intent is more powerful than demographics, according to Google's VP of Marketing, Lisa Gevelber. "Demographics rarely tell the whole story," Gevelber once wrote. "Understanding consumer intent is much more powerful."

Content mapping should always take intent into consideration. When designing your content map, you have to figure out why anyone would want to download that white paper or read your latest blog post. What is the current state of mind of the ideal consumer who would read that email? What value or knowledge resources can you provide to help address their concerns?

2. **Tailor Strategy to the Unique Attributes of Each Channel**

Format is one of the most undervalued qualities of a good content map. By format, I mean the packaging of your content (e.g. blog posts, white papers, and case studies). Every stage of the buying process calls for a unique level of engagement.

For instance, a customer shopping for new cars is not ready to test drive your cars in the awareness stage of his journey. He has just become aware of the fact that he needs a new car and wants to narrow down the list and maybe even read a few vehicle reviews before visiting your shop. Keep format in mind when structuring your content roadmap, as it can help drive the necessary conversations you need to keep customers engaged.

3. **Track, Measure and Optimize**

How will success be measured? Metrics give you a window to your progress. Determine the key performance indicators that will help you understand how your content strategy is performing at every point in the process.

Metrics will depend on content format and marketing goals. For example, if your goal is to create a webinar to generate business leads, you want to measure the number of webinar registrations. You may also want to send a post-event email and measure the engagement levels of webinar participants, as well as the participant-to-lead conversion ratio.

MIND THE GAP

1. Review your content strategy.
2. Note if any relevant channel is missing.
3. Make a plan on how to plug the gap.

9

A COMPELLING OFFER

"People don't want to buy a quarter-inch drill; they want a quarter-inch hole."
Theodore Levitt
(Professor, Harvard Business School)

There you are, at the mountain top. You've been gathering tools. Collecting maps. And now, you're ready to see what lies ahead. So, you swing your backpack around, reach inside and retrieve your binoculars. What do you see? What's your reason to believe?

When your customers look at your landing page, what do they see at the top of the mountain? What's their reason to believe? As a marketer, you must offer your customer something in exchange for their time. This is your offer.

What is an Offer?

An offer is the customer's prize for trusting you with his time and money. It's the reason a customer takes the necessary first step to buy your product or subscribe to your service. It's what awaits him on the other end of the click.

Here are some examples of offers:
- A discount coupon
- A free resource
- A free trial
- A demo
- A free consultation
- A sample of your product or service

Three Common Offer Mistakes to Avoid

Marketing is full of spaghetti offers. I call them spaghetti offers because people are throwing ideas like spaghetti on the wall to see what sticks. Unless you buy your spaghetti from Gorilla Glue, it probably won't stick.

Here are the three common offer mistakes to avoid:

1. **Lack of a clear benefit**

   If you don't state the clear benefit of your offer, it's much more difficult to stand out in a noisy world. Start with why. Lead with a clear benefit. Spell it out as explicitly and specifically as possible. It's worth the extra effort to articulate the value of your offer, because it could be the difference between a back button and a sale.

2. **Lack of credibility**

   If it's not clear why customers should trust your offer, they will simply say, "No, thanks." Use credibility signals to show that you are trustworthy and believable. Credibility signals include customer testimonials, relevant industry accolades, and *verifiable* qualifications. Go ahead, show off. Brag a little. This is your moment to shine.

3. **Inadequate offer mapping**

You could create the world's most interesting offer, but if it's not mapped to the right persona and at the right stage, it's not likely to resonate. An example of poor offer mapping is asking for a sale too soon. Lily is browsing the web for a list of financial instruments, but she's not necessarily ready for a free private appointment with a wealth advisor. So, a pay-per-click ad targeting Lily solely for appointments will likely result in waste. Instead, it would be better to offer her a free guide with detailed explanation of the various financial instruments. Then, when she's ready to talk to an advisor, the offer comes in just at the right time.

The Purpose of an Offer

Every offer you create should seek to fulfill a specific purpose. There are two primary applications to consider:

1. **Lead Generation**

This type of offer exists to generate leads. It provides your customer with valuable information or education. In exchange, you earn permission to continue the conversation. A lead generation offer helps bridge the gap between sales and marketing.

By incentivizing the lead pipeline with an offer, you are better positioned to build trust and nurture your customer relationship.

For example, a customer shopping for an engagement ring could benefit from a free guide on how to know what type of ring his partner wants. This customer is not yet ready to buy, but when he is, he will remember the company that provided such a useful guide. A lead generation offer is best mapped to a customer in the awareness and research stages of the journey.

2. A Sale

The purchase offer simply asks for a sale. This type of offer is best mapped to a customer in the conversion phase of the journey. It could be a discount, a warranty, or a trial that converts to a final sale.

For example, a customer considering dental cleaning sees an offer that offers free teeth whitening for new patients. The customer thinks, "Oh, that would be useful after I get my teeth cleaned."

How to Develop a Compelling Offer

People have different needs as they move through different stages of the buying process. Your offer should evolve to match their intent and scenario. As the customer learns more and gains confidence, your offer should increase with significance and urgency.

Case Study: Personalizing the Offer

When I led the digital marketing program at Equipment Depot, our team launched a campaign promoting a forklift brand that was superior to the competition. Our messaging was always contextual.

When reaching out to our primary persona, the procurement manager, we focused on cost savings. We showed a simple math that illustrated the benefits of our product over the alternative. Procurement managers are evaluated on helping companies secure great deals without compromising quality. So, we focused on how our product could help make them the hero.

With our secondary persona, the warehouse manager, we went in a different direction. We highlighted efficiency and performance benefits. Cost was secondary to warehouse managers. While they contributed to the purchasing decision, they were not ultimately responsible for buying the equipment. They focused primarily on issues like safety, performance, and productivity. Again, we sought to match our offer to their motivators.

With both audiences, it made sense to promote a warranty. Procurement had an extra incentive to buy. Warehouse managers had peace of mind that the equipment would be durable.

The campaign was incredibly successful, helping the company increase awareness, leads, and marketing-generated revenue.

Your offer and your messaging go hand in hand. Make sure both are mapped according to what matters to your personas.

Consider Hidden Benefits

A hidden benefit is a motivator that is separate but connected to your primary offer. This is, essentially, a silent motivator. The hidden benefit is a dominant thought on your persona's mind. Conscious or unconscious, it's always present.

When crafting an offer, look for opportunities to satisfy one or more of the following appeals:

1. Wealth
2. Wisdom
3. Pride

Here are some specific examples of hidden benefits:

1. To have more free time
2. To be more attractive
3. To impress friends and family
4. To make more friends
5. To be liked by others
6. To be pain-free
7. To be happier

Customers don't want a product or a service; they want a solution. This is what Professor Levitt meant when he said, "People don't want to buy a quarter-inch drill; they want a quarter-inch hole."

The opportunity is to identify the genuine, unstated, emotional appeal underneath your offer. This may require some circuitous messaging, but it will inevitably increase your chances of connecting with your audience.

So, how do you know if you have a compelling offer?

You probably have a compelling offer if the answer to one or more of the following is yes:

- Is it one of a kind?
- Is it exclusive?
- Is it urgent?
- Is it trustworthy?
- Is the value of the offer greater than the cost of engagement?

What If I Don't Have Anything to Offer?

Sometimes, it seems like there is nothing valuable to offer. If this describes your situation, consider the possibility that there is something to offer. You simply haven't found it yet.

Start by taking stock of all the features and benefits of your product or service. Then, brainstorm with your team or agency to discuss the best way to incentivize your audience.

The goal here is to focus on benefits and transformative outcomes, as opposed to technical features. As Simon Sinek famously said in his Golden Circle TED Talk, people don't buy what you do, they buy why you do it.

Go a step further. Go beyond the why of what you do and lean into the why of the customer's needs. Why should they take your offer? Is it because it brings them closer to a solution? Is it because it promises a transformation?

Troubleshooting Your Offer

A great offer isn't always enough to do the trick. People have all sorts of objections to products and services. Don't take it personally.

If more than 90% of your customers are rejecting your offer, figure out why. What are their objections? Are the steps clearly spelled out? Are you selling hamburger to vegetarians? Did you use the right delivery system? Maybe your email offer could be best delivered via direct mail. Does the offer sound too good to be true? Are you using credibility signals? Are you creating too much friction?

Perhaps, you could increase conversion with a few small tweaks. For example, you may offer a money-back guarantee.

Whatever the objections, be honest in your evaluation. As Ray Dalio once said, "To be effective, you must not let your need to be right be more important than your need to find out what's true." An unsuccessful offer is a chance to find out what went wrong and fix it.

ON A PLATTER

Develop a conceptual offer to promote your business. Incorporate at least one hidden appeal.

10

SUCCESS METRICS

"Every line is the perfect length if you don't measure it."
Marty Rubin
(Author, *The Boiled Frog Syndrome*)

There is a pervasive myth, usually promoted by doubters, that you can't measure content marketing. It's a lie, of course. With the right tools and processes, you can measure the impact of content on your marketing program.

You can gauge whether your content is resonating or not. Here are some questions to ponder, when measuring content:

- Are people engaging with my offer in the awareness stage?
- Are they ultimately buying or requesting quotes?
- Which 20% of my content is converting 80% of my customers?

The key to making all this work is good data—and the ability to analyze and act on it. Start by setting goals and objectives. This allows you to measure your progress against the stated objectives.

Here are a couple of ways to analyze your goals:

1. Measure your success in the context of lead generation (for example, inquiries, newsletter subscriptions, and quote requests)
2. Measure your success in the context of revenue goals (for example, customer acquisition, sales, and marketing-generated revenue)

Benchmarking

Start by taking stock of where your content is today. Benchmark your report based on current traffic and leads generated from your content marketing program. Using this benchmark, you'll start to get a better idea of how your content mapping strategy is impacting your progress.

Competitive Landscaping

Your competitors can be a good reference point for performance. Create a competitive landscape that includes your primary and secondary competitors and monitor their content. Add a third landscape to track tertiary or influencer competitors—these can be companies outside your industry whose content you admire. Pay attention to their content mapping strategies. You never know where inspiration might come from.

Content Marketing Metrics

According to the Content Marketing Institute, the following are the most trusted content metrics used by B2C and B2B marketers:

- Website traffic
- Social media shares
- Time spent on website
- Sales
- Conversion rates
- SEO ranking
- Subscriber growth
- Sales lead quality

Narrative Labels

A *narrative label* is a simple tag that identifies an audience or category. Content can be categorized by using narrative labels. Each label can be used to represent a persona, a topic or a stage in the buyer's journey.

Create narrative labels, then assign them accordingly. Your narrative label reflects the impact of your content. Measure your mix of content to track the pull of each label.

Let's say you have a persona who is a parent looking for air purification solutions. You might create some social media posts promoting the benefits of your product. Use a narrative label to track how well this type of content is performing by measuring reach and resonance.

Labels are great for tracking the stages of the buyer's journey. For example, if you're curious about how well your awareness content is performing on social media, label it on your content calendar. Some social media tools are equipped with tagging capabilities. If your tool allows for tagging, use narrative labels to organize your tagging system.

Measure your labels monthly to track content engagement. For instance, you could tag each piece of content by labeling it after a persona or a stage in the buying process. Then, measure all your labels to see which ones are resonating the most.

You can also use narrative labels to track topics. For example, if you are trying to broaden your messaging on sustainability, you'll simply tag each related post under your "Sustainability" label. Then, review your report every 30 days to see how well it's performing.

Go Retro

If you're feeling extra motivated, go back and tag old content. You'll get a good picture of how your content has performed over time and what types of content are still performing well. *If it ain't broke, don't break it.*

Measurement by Channel

When it comes to content mapping, we're mostly interested in seeing how content can help customers take the next step. To that effect, our metrics must reflect engagement and conversion rates across all channels. Depending on the channel in play, different metrics will apply.

Website

Conversion rate: Define how many people took you up on your offers since you installed your content mapping program.

A conversion may include:
- lead form completion
- quote request
- resource download
- mailing list subscription
- social media follow

If your landing page conversion went from 20% to 50%, it's a sign that your content is resonating.

Engagement rate: Engagement can be measured by tracking time spent on your website (should be higher) or bounce rate (should be lower). If people are interacting with more content, such as longer video viewing sessions or more time spent playing with widgets and calculators, these are all signs of higher engagement.

Those are the two most relevant metrics related to content, but there are other important website performance indicators, including:
- Pages viewed per session
- Search queries
- Events
- Unique sessions
- Exit pages

Email

Remember, email is a conversation channel. The conversation usually follows a sequence. The first sequence is to get a reader to open your email. The next step is to bring them to your landing page, if you're using one.

It makes sense that these are the two most important metrics to track:

Open Rate: This measures the number of people who opened your email. An open rate of 25% is solid.

Click-through Rate: This is the percentage of people who opened and clicked your email. A CTR of 3% is considered average.

Other email metrics to keep an eye on include:

- Deliverability rate
- Conversion rate
- Bounce rate
- Marked as spam
- Unsubscribes

Social Media

Social media metrics are about reach, resonance, and conversion. You want to measure the increase in user engagement (reach), user conversations and shares (resonance), and desired actions from social media (conversion).

Be sure to track the following:

Impressions: Number of times a user saw your content. This shows the reach of your content.

Engagement: This metric defines how many people engaged with your content. An engagement unit can be a like, sentiment, or share.

Participation: Useful participation signals are comments and replies.

Audience: As your content starts to reach more relevant customers, your number of followers should reflect your progress. This is worth tracking at least once a month.

Conversion: Likes and comments are great, but without a conversion there is no sale. Keep an eye on the number of conversions generated by your social media pages.

Paid Search

It's important to measure your paid ads, considering they can be expensive if not closely monitored.

Cost Per Acquisition: This is the average amount it costs you to acquire a customer.

Click-through Rate: This is the percentage of people who saw your ad and clicked on it. A higher CTR is an indication of relevant content.

Conversion Rate: This is the average number of conversions per ad click. The formula is the number of conversions divided by total ad clicks.

Organic Search

As you create more focused, relevant and helpful content, pay attention to your search rankings. Keep an eye on the following SEO metrics:

1. **Keyword ranking change**: This tracks your keyword positioning on search engines. The closer to the first position the better. Most users do not click past the first page.

2. **Conversion rate from organic**: This measures the percentage of people who completed a conversion action after finding you through a web search.

What Are We Looking For?

When analyzing data, pay attention to patterns, whether positive or negative. Ask questions.

For example:

1. What are the trends?
2. What changed?
3. How is the new content performing?
4. What's my hypothesis?
5. How can I test?
6. Is there an opportunity to A/B test (e.g. two different subject lines or offers)?

Brainstorm with your team and generate different ideas. The goal is to formulate hypotheses from the brainstorming session. Test your ideas and document the changes.

Key Takeaways

- The companies that will benefit most from content mapping will know their highest-value personas, what content those potential customers are consuming, and, ultimately, where they are in their buying journey, and what additional information they need to take the next step.
- Businesses that adopt a content mapping strategy will also regularly tune their marketing tactics based on the unprecedented insight into their customer needs, made possible by honing this approach.

Five Ways to Win with Data

1. **Create a culture of measurement**. Make it a point to create a culture of clear, transparent reporting. Even if it's bad news, get used to it. Take it on the chin. Brace yourself, then get back up and go again.
2. **Design content experiments**. Get excited about the prospect of testing new hypotheses and experiments. Look for opportunities to A/B test your email, social media ads or landing pages. Don't change it wholesale. Start with small tweaks, like changing the headlines, image, or call to action.
3. **Set up content tracking *before* each campaign**. Setting up tracking in advance will make it easier to get complete data from your campaigns. It's more painful to retrofit your measurement.

4. **Map your marketing reports to your personas**. Executives prefer high-level reports that focus on business results (e.g. correlation between website traffic and lead conversions, revenue increases related to content). Leave the more granular reports for your marketing team.

5. **Make content marketing part of your overall marketing objectives**. Focus on how your content mapping strategy can help your business grow.

PACKAGED GOODS

Brainstorm 5 narrative labels for your business. Remember, labels could apply to personas, topics or stages of the buyer's journey.

THOUGHTS & ACTIONS

If you want to buy a car, you start with a thought ("I need a new car"). If you want to switch bank accounts, you start with a thought ("I need a new bank account"). If you want to replace your tortilla toaster, you start with a thought ("I need a new tortilla toaster"). This internal conversation is the initial thought that triggers the process necessary to convert thought to action.

The marketer anticipates these thoughts and the actions that follow. Guided by a content map, the marketer lays out in clear terms the path customers typically travel to discover a solution (the right bank, car or tortilla toaster).

It goes further. The map offers a guideline for creating the content most likely to speak to a customer at every stage of the buying process. Content mapping is the doorway to marketing that transforms the mundane and mediocre into the relevant and remarkable.

Content Mapping in Action

Experience has taught me that content marketing without a process is chaos. Content works better when there's an established process for repeatable success.

I've tried many iterations of content workflows, and here is the one I've found to be most effective. It's a simple 7-step process you can copy wholesale or tweak to fit your business:

Step 1: Identify a marketing opportunity

Step 2: Create a content brief to get aligned on goals and objectives

Step 3: Develop your personas, prioritizing primary & secondary personas

Step 4: Create your buyer's journey for each persona

Step 5: Design your content map for each persona

Step 6: Establish success metrics and implement tracking

Step 7: Launch your campaign

Wash. Rinse. Repeat.

CHECK ENGINE LIGHT

Your car needs an occasional tune-up to run well. Likewise, your content map needs routine maintenance to keep producing positive results. Revisit your personas and your content map at least once a quarter to make sure their needs still hold true. As you receive new inputs from your organization and the marketplace, adapt your personas and strategies accordingly.

A Content Mapping Checklist

- » Who is this content for?
- » Where are they in the buying journey?
- » What keeps them up at night?
- » What problem can I help them solve?
- » What's their path to the solution?
- » What's the best way to deliver the solution?
- » How can I meet my customers where they are?
- » Why should they care?

Coda

No one *owns* customers. We only *earn* the right to take care of them for some time. I hope that reading this book brings you a step closer to taking care of yours with joy.

Gratitude

I'm here today because of the support of the kind souls who saw potential in me. I'm grateful to Pam Lockard, whose mentorship and teachings helped transform my life. I owe at least a crate of apples to Aleesha Worthington for being a shining light in my career. Thank you to Carl Chery, Chris Gray and Brian Wallace for taking a chance on me.

Thank you for your unconditional friendship and cheerleading: Dimieari Birabi, Cindy Arzola, Kavachi, Jima, Kingsley "Rukus" Okafor, Ogochukwu "SB" Adaikpoh, Laura Dodds, Thu Nguyen, Loretta Faluade, Lolu Omotosho, Charlissa Holman, Joseph Kang.

Thank you for being a source of light and generosity: Shea Serrano, Larami, David Turner, Fat Tony, kris ex, Oliver Wang, Tara Blagg, Alan Spackman, Andy Rich, Mario Sanchez, Michelle Ngome, Marco Torres, Henry Dillard, Sama'an Ashrawi, Rolando Rodriguez, Eunice Okogbue, John Nwoke, Josh Belland, Maisha Fennell, Allyson Hill, Preemo, Jeff Cashless, Hami Arrington, Stephen Brent May, DeAndre Wright, Monique Crump, Emily Mouton, Christine Schneider, Nnanna Otuonye, Saba Soheili, Rick Celeita, Vaughn Walters, Veronica Stapleton, Farrah Akhtar, Megan Willis, Anne Schaeddel, Fatimat Villanueva, Chichi Okogbue, Wunmi Adungba, Pam Morisse, Florence Anyanwu, Uloma Chiakwelu, Banji, Precious, Stephen Cole, Tiffany Wiley, Alyssa Najar, Dani Hernandez, Amy Vernon, Nneka Kanu, Nzinga Tchameni, Felice LaZae, Idris Ayeni.

And thank you to: Rabia Ilahi, Melanie Wallace, William Ketchum III, Brandon Caldwell, Shannon Carpenter, Bill Bentley, Ore Ayodele, Meredith Nudo, NerdLine, Carrie Whittington, Brandi Lee, Alison Conteh, Steve Wilson, Chris McCarthy, Rhonda Birabi, Joëlle Rāwr, Estela Cisneros, Bobby Rigg, Jason Cunningham, Walker Robinson, Megan Burks, Taylor Wiley, Salam Nabulsi, my entire CEMEX family (there are too many of you to name), Tiffani Walker, Erika Akpan, Karissa Hubbard, the Belle Station WhatsApp Group (I'm rooting for all of you), Mich De L'Orme, Salim, Saheed, Promise, TRU Nation.

Finally, thank you to: Mom, Dad, Henry Jr., Pancake, and the other 500 people I forgot because it's 1:39 a.m. and my memory is blinking red.

It's been a joy to write this book for you.

Thank you.

About the Author

Henry Adaso is a storyteller. With an eye for opportunity and a natural ability to cast his clients as heroes, Henry drives measurable marketing results for small businesses, entrepreneurs and Fortune 500 companies alike.

With 15+ years on both the agency and client side of marketing initiatives, Henry knows how to connect the dots between C-suite priorities and audience needs to produce data-driven content, resulting in millions of dollars in marketing-generated revenue.

Before finding his home in marketing, Henry honed his knack for storycraft as a music journalist, writing for *VIBE*, *LA Weekly*, *Dotdash*, and *The Houston Press*.

You can find him at *henryadaso.com*.

For your free content mapping workbook, visit henryadaso.com/contentmapping.

www.ingramcontent.com/pod-product-compliance
Lightning Source LLC
LaVergne TN
LVHW041215050326
832903LV00021B/638